SUPER BOWL CHAMPIONS
CHICAGO BEARS

SUPER BOWL CHAMPIONS
CHICAGO BEARS

AARON FRISCH

CREATIVE EDUCATION

Published by Creative Education
P.O. Box 227, Mankato, Minnesota 56002
Creative Education is an imprint of The Creative Company
www.thecreativecompany.us

Design and production by Blue Design
Art direction by Rita Marshall
Printed in the United States of America

Photographs by Alamy (David Ball), AP Images (AP
Photo), Corbis (Bettmann), Getty Images (Lee Balterman/
Sports Illustrated, Tom Dahlin, Jonathan Daniel, Focus
on Sport, Jed Jacobsohn, Kidwiler Collection/Diamond
Images, Don Lansu, Al Messerschmidt/NFL, Ronald C.
Modra/Sports Imagery, Robert Riger, Vic Stein/NFL
Photos, Rob Tringali/SportsChrome)

Library of Congress Cataloging-in-Publication Data
Frisch, Aaron.
Chicago Bears / Aaron Frisch.
p. cm. — (Super bowl champions)
Includes index.
Summary: An elementary look at the Chicago Bears
professional football team, including its formation in 1920,
most memorable players, Super Bowl championship, and
stars of today.
ISBN 978-1-60818-373-9
1. Chicago Bears (Football team)—History—Juvenile
literature. I. Title.

GV956.C5F74 2013
796.332'640977311—dc23   2013010465

9 8 7 6 5 4 3 2

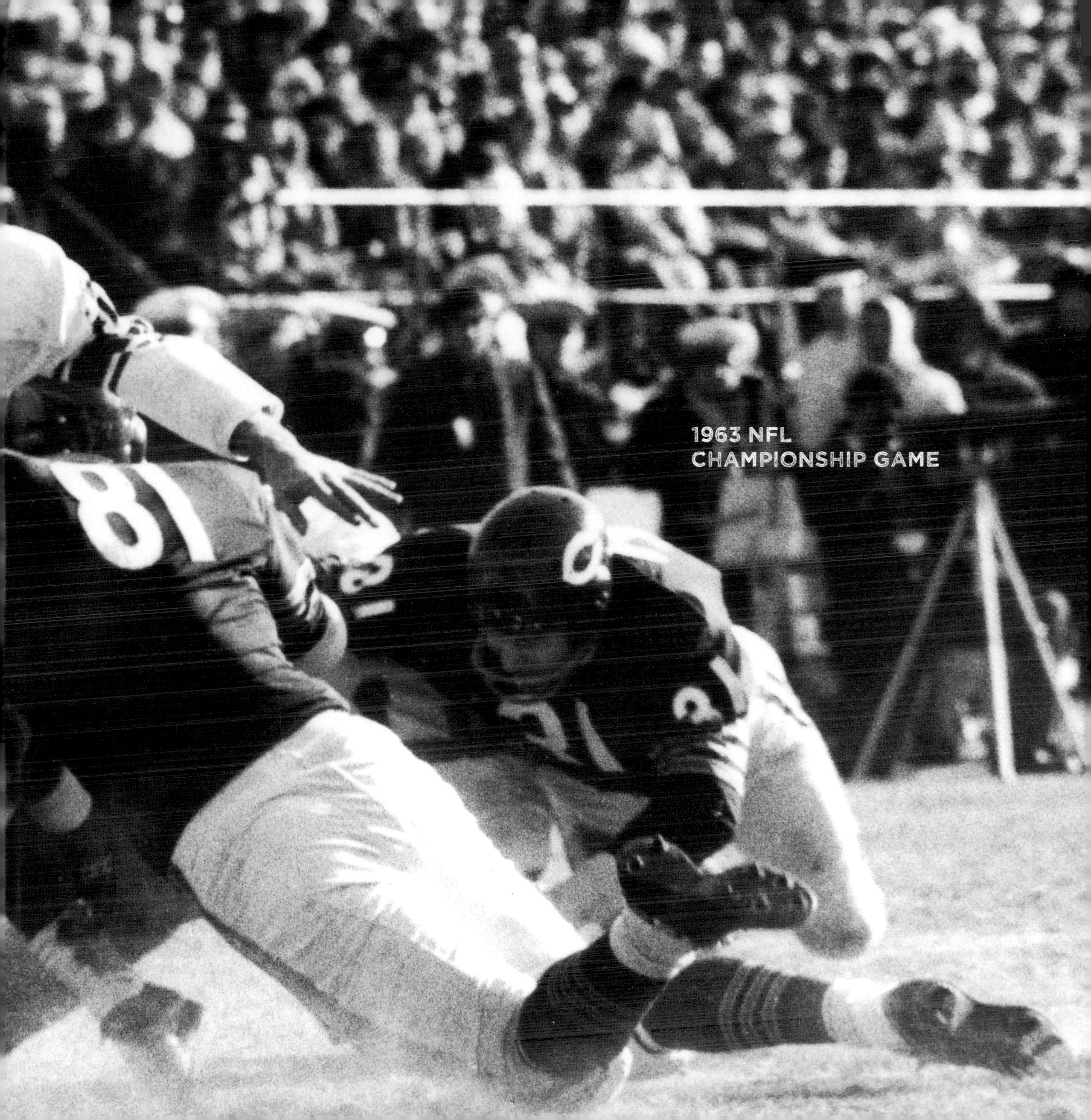
1963 NFL
CHAMPIONSHIP GAME

DICK BUTKUS / 1965–73

Dick was a linebacker during a time when the Bears were not very good. He hit so hard it was scary!

TABLE OF CONTENTS

BRONKO NAGURSKI / 1930–37, 1943

Bronko was a huge, powerful running back. He often blocked for the speedy Red Grange.

NAGURSKI: *nuh-GER-skee*

THE ROARING BEARS

Chicago, Illinois, has a baseball team called the Cubs. In 1921, Chicago got a football team, too. The owners wanted it to have a name like Cubs but fiercer. The Bears were born!

FAMOUS BEARS

RED GRANGE / 1925, 1929–34

Red was Chicago's first star running back. He was so hard to catch that he was called the "Galloping Ghost."

BRIAN URLACHER

2000–12

Brian was a linebacker who was both big and fast. He tackled hard like Dick Butkus used to.

URLACHER: *ER-lak-er*

MONSTERS OF THE MIDWAY

The Chicago Bears have had some of the best running backs and linebackers in National Football League (NFL) history. Fans call the Bears the "Monsters of the Midway"!

"If God had wanted man to play soccer, he wouldn't have given us arms."
—MIKE DITKA

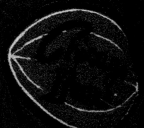

"Nothing is work unless you'd rather be doing something else."

—GEORGE HALAS

THE BEARS' STORY

George Halas owned and coached the Bears when they started playing in Chicago. Chicago won the NFL championship three times in the 1920s and 1930s.

Quarterback Sid Luckman led Chicago to four more **titles** in the 1940s. The Bears played some exciting games against their **rivals**, the Green Bay Packers.

SID LUCKMAN

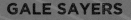

GALE SAYERS

Chicago won another championship in 1963. The Bears lost a lot of games after that, even though they had fast running back Gale Sayers.

In the 1980s, the Bears got better. They beat the New England Patriots 46–10 in Super Bowl XX (20). It was the biggest Super Bowl blowout ever!

WALTER PAYTON / 1975–87

Walter was a running back who carried the ball for 16,726 total yards. That set a new NFL **record**.

RUNNING BACK MATT FORTE

DEVIN HESTER

The Bears played in another Super Bowl after the 2006 season. Wide receiver Devin Hester scored a touchdown for Chicago on the first kickoff. But the Bears lost.

uarterback Jay Cutler led Chicago's offense in 2013. He could fire passes far down the field. Jay and his teammates hoped to roar back to a Super Bowl soon!

"It goes back to the offensive line, it starts and stops with those guys."

—JAY CUTLER

MIKE SINGLETARY / 1981-92

Mike was a very smart linebacker. After he quit playing football, he became an NFL coach.

GLOSSARY

record — something that is the most or best ever

rivals — teams that play extra hard against each other

skyscrapers — tall, narrow buildings that have at least 10 stories, or levels

titles — in sports, another word for championships

INDEX